Foreword

At GenMove, we believe that every child deserves a healthy lifestyle. That every child can contribute to a team. And that every child should experience the thrill of being physically active – regardless of innate ability, past experiences, or physical limitations.

We've designed innovative activities and inclusive, non-threatening equipment that will level the playing field to ensure that all students can experience the benefits of physical activity.

This Adapted Physical Education Activity Book contains the tools you need to incorporate GenMove activities into your classroom and engage students in active learning. Each developmentally appropriate, inclusive activity includes student learning objectives, skills to be learned, equipment needs, set-up diagrams and instructions, and suggested modifications. We have provided general strategies for inclusion in any setting as well as guidelines for modifying activities for students with specific disabilities. The curriculum also includes teacher and student authentic assessment activities that demonstrate student learning given NASPE's Standards.

Whether you use this curriculum as a starting point or an enhancement of your Adapted Physical Education programming, we wish you and your students many hours of active play, inclusion, and learning.

Acknowledgements

The development of educational programming is a collaborative effort. We would like to thank the many instructors and students who have assisted us in field-testing and refining our activities.

We particularly wish to thank and acknowledge Dr. Joanne Margaret Hynes-Hunter of Dr. Joanne Hunter, LLC, for her contributions in the creation of this curriculum.

Contents

What is Adapted Physical Education?

Adapted physical education (APE) ensures that students with a wide range of disabilities and needs will meet the goals and standards of the regular physical education program. That is, each student with a disability will experience success in a safe environment, thus gaining the physical, social, and psychological benefits that a quality physical education program offers.

In APE, the teacher adapts or modifies the curriculum, task, equipment, and/or environment (creating what is known as the "least restrictive environment") so that students can participate in physical education along with their peers. Students are given appropriate placement within the least restrictive environment in accordance with Public Law (P.L.) 94-142 (Education of All Handicapped Children Act), now codified as IDEA (Individuals with Disabilities Education Act, P.L. 101-476) in 1990, and the subsequent reauthorization of the law in 1997. This means that physical education needs to be provided to students with a disability as part of the students' education in order to learn how to interact effectively with their environment and use their leisure time wisely.

Teachers need to ensure that students with disabilities develop physical and motor fitness, fundamental motor skills and patterns, and dance/aquatics/sports skills so they can participate in community-based leisure, recreation and sports activities and enjoy an enhanced quality of life. Students with disabilities should be seen as students first.

The most effective way to provide quality physical education to students with disabilities is the same as for students without disabilities. All students, regardless of ability level, need to be challenged to achieve, encouraged to try, praised for their success, and involved in decision-making. However, modifying instruction for students with disabilities is not always easy.

Unfortunately, many regular physical education teachers are not equipped with the knowledge and skills to effectively include students with disabilities into their classes, while special education teachers may face the challenges of working with students with different disabilities in the same room. Therefore, the information that follows offers basic information and general strategy suggestions to help make planning and teaching a little easier – so that all students, regardless of their abilities, can succeed.

Suggestions For Adapting Activities

Adaptations need to be specific to each individual student based on his/her abilities. However, there are many general modifications that can be applied to students with similar needs. A few suggestions are listed below.

When Giving Rules, Prompts, & Cues:

- Show and tell (talk about and demonstrate) all directions when teaching a new skill or introducing how to play a game.
- Use peers as partners.
- Shorten time limits.
- Give oral prompts reminding students what they need to do and/or how to do it.
- Provide more space between students (give them room).
- Allow ball to remain stationary (especially for kicking and striking activities).
- Place the student with a disability near the teacher so the student can see and hear the teacher more clearly.
- Allow students to carry the ball in lap (if in wheelchair) or allow students with limited mobility/balance to sit in a chair when throwing/catching a ball.
- Remove the competitive aspects of the activity. This will slow the activity down and put less stress on the students.
- Decrease the number of repetitions a student with disabilities has to do (or increase the amount for the student without a disability to keep the activity "even").
- Emphasize process of movement (good basketball throw) over product (number of points scored or accuracy).
- Use a beeper or radio behind the goal for individual with visual impairment.
- Keep directions simple.
- Use immediate and positive feedback.
- Be flexible and improvise as needed.

When Creating Boundaries for the Activity Space:

- Decrease distance between the goal and how far the students have to travel.
- Use well-defined boundaries (use equipment with bright or sharp contrast of colors, or with raised edges).
- Adapt play area (make boundary space smaller or remove obstacles as needed).
- Simplify station pattern rotations and use arrows on the floor for students to use as visual cues indicating where to move next.

When Selecting Equipment:

- Use larger and/or lighter equipment.
- Use scoops (or 1-gallon milk containers or similar large plastic containers with the bottom cut off) to make catching/throwing easier.
- Use Velcro straps to increase control and grip when holding equipment.
- Mark positions on playing field with polyspots or an "X" so students know where to stand or where to move back to.
- Vary the size, weight, color, and texture of balls. For example, use beach balls, balloons (be aware of latex allergies), balls made up of crumpled paper, foam balls, yarn balls, balls made out of duct tape or masking tape, mesh (shower) balls, rolled socks (sewn closed), Nerf balls, Wiffle balls, and garbage bag balls (fill a garbage bag with inflated balloons).

When Students are Engaged in the Activity:

- Change locomotor skills and patterns. (Walking, jogging, running, and crawling in a straight line are generally easier locomotor skills and patterns. Hopping, skipping, and jumping in curved or zigzag patterns are generally more difficult.)
- Modify body positions. (In order to be successful at a skill, students may benefit from sitting down on the floor or in a chair.)
- Modify grasps.
- Reduce number of actions or steps.
- Lengthen or shorten the time of an activity based on the student's needs. (Student may need time lengthened in order to accomplish a task, or time may need to be shortened because the student does not have the endurance for long periods of activity.)
- Provide frequent rest periods.

- Build a skill sequence: mirror each skill when teaching; break skills down into very small parts and teach those parts, keeping instruction simple; use teacher or peer assistance with movement as the student requires (do not assume the student needs help all the time).

- Slow down the activity pace as needed.

- When rolling a ball: Have the student use two hands instead of one; allow student to remain in stationary position (moving and performing a skill is most difficult); have student use a ramp to roll the ball down toward a target; use a partner if the student requires one; remove armrests (only if it is safe to do so) to give the student more mobility; and have students with limited balance or mobility roll a ball from a sitting position on a chair.

- When throwing/catching: Use Velcro balls and mitts; have students with limited balance/mobility throw and catch from a sitting position on a chair; to aid in throwing the ball, allow a sitting student to push the ball off a ramp, from the lap, or from a tee; use beeper balls for those with visual impairments; provide a peer to assist if needed; if students are unable to throw, allow them to kick the ball toward another player; and remove armrests (only if it is safe to do so) to give the student more mobility.

- When striking: Use larger (barrels) or smaller (in length) bats; use a batting tee (or extra large cone or bucket to place the ball on). Bats may be foam noodles, pillow polo sticks (a long handled implement with a large, soft barrel), or paddles with large faces, thicker handles, and/or attached hand straps.

- When kicking: Use large, light balls (balloons, beach balls) for the student in a wheelchair or using a walker or crutches; tether a ball to the wheelchair using elastic; place beanbags on student's feet and tell the student to try and kick it off; remove foot plates on wheelchairs (when appropriate); slightly deflate the balls; and kick a stationary ball first and progress to a ball that is moving.

Assisting Students with Specific Disabilities:

The following basic strategies may be used when working with students with certain categories of disability:

Visual Impairments:

- Position student close to the teacher.
- Orient persons to the room using specifics like "clock clues" (e.g. "The goal is at the 12 O' Clock position.").
- Do not shout.

- Give verbal cues when talking (e.g. "When performing the soccer chip shot, kick the ball using the laces of the sneaker…" and NOT "Watch how I perform the soccer chip shot and then do it on your own…").
- Identify yourself and others around you (especially when first entering a room or being introduced).
- Do not leave without saying you are doing so.

Speech Impairments:

- Give your whole attention to the person.
- Allow time for person to finish speaking.
- Ask short questions that require short answers, and speak normally.
- Speak expressively.
- Use pen/paper if needed.
- Don't pretend to understand when you do not.

Deaf or Hard of Hearing:

- Look at the student and speak clearly, slowly, and expressively, with normal tone.
- Position student close to the teacher.
- Keep instructions, directions, and expectations simple.
- Get student's full attention before talking.
- Allow the student to move around the activity area during instruction so s/he chooses the position to best see and hear the teacher or another student who may be talking.
- While giving instructions, turn off fans, air conditioners, music, and other sources of noise.
- Keep verbal directions short and to the point and include a visual demonstration.
- When introducing a new concept, print it on a poster board or handout.
- Use captioned movies and instructional videos.
- Allow students to ask for directions to be repeated.
- Use pen and paper if needed.
- Place the person who is talking near a light source.

- When talking, do not cover your mouth.
- Talk directly to the person who is deaf or hard of hearing, not the interpreter.
- If you are writing a message, do not talk at the same time.

Orthopedic Impairments:

- Don't move a person's assistive device without permission.
- Speak at their eye level, but do not kneel.
- When giving directions, consider distance, terrain, or obstacles.
- Be aware that students with severe motor delays may have difficulty with positional concepts such as "up, down, over, under" as they have not been able to actively and independently move their bodies in relation to their environment and so have not internalized these concepts.
- Make the environment and activity accessible. This is vital for participation. Things such as increasing target size may be needed. Be aware that quick, fast movements may increase spasticity, while slow, rhythmical movement may decrease tone.

Autism/Asperger's Syndrome/Cognitive:

- Allow time for the individual to learn and master a new task (repetition is important).
- Give one direction at a time.
- Keep instructions, directions, and expectations simple.
- Focus on basic fundamental skill progression.
- Be patient and allow extra time for the person to put his/her thoughts together.
- Give exact and detailed directions and instructions (i.e. "We will play this round until 12:30" as opposed to "1 minute").
- Students with autism often have sensory issues such as sensitivity to noise, light, or touch and gravitational insecurity, so be sensitive and respectful to sensory issues when planning activities.
- Be aware of behaviors and what the student is trying to communicate through those behaviors.
- Autistic students learn best through visual channels. Demonstrations, combined with pictures, are more effective than verbal cues alone.

Down Syndrome:

- Students with Down syndrome have low tone in their hands, as well as the rest of their body. The bones of the hand do not fully develop until ages 8-9. This makes tasks requiring fine hand coordination difficult. Thus, ball skills may be challenging.

- Students often have heart conditions that may or may not have been remediated. Therefore, be careful when engaging in cardiovascular activities.

- Students have decreased strength and motor coordination. Therefore, general strength and endurance activities are areas to improve.

- Repetition of a task, until it is mastered, is important.

- Breaking the task down into smaller components is often effective.

Teaching Aids

Many students with disabilities are not able to read or use handouts or materials that are typically given out. Below is information on a variety of alternate formats that might be used.

Large Print

- Double space text, and use 1-inch margins on all sides.

- Use a bold serif 16 font for text, non-bold serif font for headings.

- Underline instead of using italics.

- Print single-sided pages.

- Use non-glare paper.

Visual Aids

- Use large visual aids with bold fonts and bright, high-contrast colors.

- Always describe visuals.

- Provide copies or outlines of the in-class lessons to bring home as needed to complete assessments.

Audio/Electronic

- Have computer disks available for homework or other assignments to be put on disks.

- Save information as a text file.

- Have audiotapes on hand with tape recorder.

- Always orally describe pictures on handouts (e.g. "The assessment shows a picture of a boy standing with his arms stretched out. The question is 'which body part is not allowed to touch the ball when playing soccer?'").

Additional Information:

American Association for Physical Activity and Recreation (AAPAR)
http://www.aahperd.org/aapar/

As an association comprised of a diverse membership of professionals, AAPAR seeks to increase public awareness, understanding, and support for lifelong and inclusive physical activity and recreation programs and to serve the profession by disseminating guidelines, standards of practice and offering continuing education in different specialized areas of practice. AAPAR's twelve member councils include the Adapted Physical Education Council comprised of and led by leaders and experts in the field of adapted physical education.

Adapted Physical Education National Standards (APENS)
http://www.apens.org

The mission of APENS is to promote the fifteen Adapted Physical Education Standards and national certification exam.

The goal of APENS is to promote a nationally certified Adapted Physical Educator (CAPE) – the one qualified person who can make meaningful decisions for children with disabilities in physical education – within every school district in the country.

Association for Physical Education
http://www.afpe.org.uk/

The Association for Physical Education provides quality assured services and resources and valuable professional support for members and the physical education and school sport profession through a range of high-quality accredited professional development opportunities, employment support, employment opportunities, regular newsletter, email and text updates, representation at key stakeholder meetings and national working parties, insurance cover and dedicated help lines for health & safety and legal advice.

National Center on Physical Activity & Disability (NCPAD):
http://www.ncpad.org

The NCPAD Web site features NCPAD's Research Citation Database, which contains references for journal articles, newsletters, book excerpts, and hyperlinks to Web sites as well as NCPAD's Fact Sheets and Bibliographies on topics relating to specific activities and disabilities. NCPAD's Web site also provides national resource directories of facilities, programs, and events concerned with physical activity and disability.

National Consortium on Physical Education and Recreation for Individuals with Disabilities (NCPERID)
http://ncperid.org/

This site is maintained by the National Consortium on Physical Education and Recreation for Individuals with Disabilities. It contains information on the Consortium's mission, annual meeting, membership information, and an on-line copy of its newsletter, "The Advocate."

PALAESTRA: Forum of Sport, Physical Education & Recreation For Those With Disabilities
http://www.palaestra.com/

This quarterly publication, published in cooperation with both the U.S. Olympic Committee's Committee on Sports for the Disabled and the American Alliance for Health, Physical Education, Recreation & Dance's Adapted Physical Activity Council, is a valuable resource for consumers, their families, and professionals in the field. PALAESTRA provides a forum for the exchange of ideas and information concerning adapted physical activity for individuals with disabilities.

PE Central
http://www.pecentral.org/adapted/adaptedmenu.html

The Web site provides information about developmentally appropriate adapted physical education practices and programs. The site includes lesson plans, videos, assessments research, products, standards, and more.

Project INSPIRE
http://www.twu.edu/inspire/

Enormous amount of information related to individuals with disabilities. Some of the information includes instructional techniques, inclusion strategies, sport organizations, health and safety issues, and even a parent page to assist with activities in the home and community.

Skill Concepts: Chasing, Fleeing, Dodging, Throwing, Striking, Kicking, Spatial awareness

Standard: NASPE Standard 1 (Competency in movement motor skills)

Equipment: 1 large goal, 1 striking implement, 3 balls per student, 1 polyspot per
student

Set Up:

1. Place the goal in the center of the activity space.
2. Put the striking implement in the goal.
3. Place the polyspots in a circle approximately 2 yards away from the goal.
4. Put 3 balls on top of each polyspot.

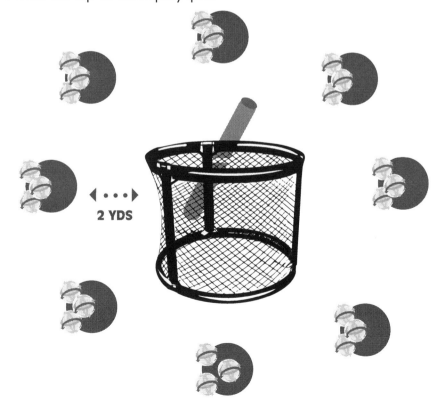

2 YDS

How To Play:

1. Chose one student to be the "Striker," and position them inside the goal.

2. Position the remaining students on the polyspots circling the goal (one student per polyspot).

3. Tell the students not to move more than one or two steps in any direction from their polyspot. If appropriate, say "Pretend you are in a bubble and that bubble is as big and far as you can stretch and reach with your body parts."

4. Give a signal for students to attempt to throw or kick the balls (your choice) into the goal from their polyspot. The Striker's objective is to keep the balls out of the goal by hitting them away with the striking implement. The Striker may move around in the inside of the goal, but may not place body parts or the striking implement across the goal to prevent scoring.

5. After all the balls are thrown, signal to the students to SAFELY retrieve 3 balls from the ground around the activity area. Have students return to their original polyspots.

6. Choose a new Striker after each round. The new Striker takes position in the goal, and the original Striker occupies the empty polyspot.

Check This Out:

1. Instead of choosing a student Striker, you can serve as Striker. This allows for eye contact with each student and increases students' goal-scoring success rate.

2. Have students count and record the number of balls in the goal for each round played. Depending on the students' cognitive level:

   - Add the totals from each round for a sum total (e.g., Round 1=10 goals; Round 2=20 goals. 10+20=30 total goals).

   - Add the totals from each round and calculate the average (Round 1=10 goals; Round 2=20 goals. 10+20=30/2=15).

   - Find the difference between each round (Round 2=20 goals; Round 1=10 goals. 20-10=10. They improved by 10 goals in Round 2.).

   - Include a scoring system where each type of ball is worth a certain number of points. For example, a GenMove ball is worth 1 point, a sock ball is worth 2 points, and a paper ball is worth 3 points.

Activity Modifications:

EASIER

1. For the Striker: add a second Striker who moves around the outside of the goal.

2. Have the students throw underhand.

3. Have the students throw/kick with their dominant (preferred) hand/foot.

4. Move students closer to the goal while keeping a safe distance from the Striker.

5. Choose equipment that is developmentally appropriate and increases student success rate, which will increase learning. For example, lightweight balls (e.g., paper or tape) thrown from a close distance may make the task easier. (However, if a ball is too light it may lack the momentum to reach the goal.)

6. Allow students to use 2 hands to hold and throw balls.

7. Let students roll the ball into the goal.

HARDER

1. Use more difficult throwing skills including overhead or sidearm.

2. Have the students throw/kick using their non-dominant (non-preferred) hand/foot.

3. Add a second Striker who moves around outside the goal to increase difficulty for other students.

4. Move the students farther away from the goal.

Ball n Goal Teacher Assessment

DIRECTIONS: Students will demonstrate competency in motor skills by achieving a score of 2 or higher for each of the 5 Ball n Goal Teacher Assessment skills.

1. Using the template below and your class roster, create and print your own personalized assessment form.

2. Observe each student while they are playing Ball n Goal to determine if the skill is performed correctly, using the rubric and listed cues for each skill to guide grading:

   - 1=Needs Improvement: cannot demonstrate the critical elements of the skill with cues from the teacher.

   - 2=Satisfactory: demonstrates the critical elements of the skill with cues from the teacher.

   - 3=Outstanding: demonstrates all of the critical elements of the skill without cues from the teacher.

3. Add comments as needed in the section provided.

Underhand Throwing

- Face target.
- If student is capable of standing: Step with opposite foot towards the target (i.e., if throwing with right hand, step towards target with left foot).
- Use a pendulum arm motion with the throwing arm (i.e., like bowling).
- Follow through with the throwing hand pointing toward the target.

Overhand Throwing

- Point non-throwing side/shoulder to the target (for example, if right handed point left shoulder/side towards target).
- Bring throwing wrist back to ear.
- If student is capable of standing: Step with opposite foot towards target (i.e., if throwing with left hand, step towards target with right foot).
- Follow through: let the throwing arm come across the opposite side of body.

Kicking

- If student is capable of standing: Place non-kicking foot next to the ball.
- Contact ball in the middle with preferred foot.
- Use the inside of the preferred foot.
- Follow through: point-kicking foot toward target.
- Use a firm kick (with power) so the ball reaches the target.

Striking

- Grip the striking implement so that hands are close together and the preferred hand is on top.
- If student is capable of standing: Stand with knees bent.
- Swing the striking implement in an effort to keep the ball from entering the goal by hitting/knocking the ball away.

Spatial Awareness (Personal Space)

- Students were told not to move more than one to two steps from the polyspot to demonstrate personal space. Does the student stay in their personal space?

TO PASS: Students must achieve a score of 2 or higher for each skill.

Student Name	Underhand Throwing	Overhand Throwing	Kicking	Striking	Spatial Awareness (Personal Space)	Comments

Ball n Goal Student Assessment

DIRECTIONS: Students will demonstrate competency in motor skills by achieving a score of 70% or higher on the Ball n Goal Student Assessment Worksheet that identifies key ski concepts learned during participating in this activity.

1. Give each student the appropriate (either lower or higher cognitively functioning student) Ball n Goal Student Assessment Worksheet and a pencil.
2. Give students time to complete and turn in the worksheet.
3. Use the Ball n Goal Student Assessment Worksheet ANSWERS to grade the student worksheets.

TO PASS:

1. Lower cognitively functioning students: Students must achieve an 80% or higher, with each correct answer worth 20%.
2. Higher cognitively functioning students: Students must achieve a 70% or higher, with each correct answer worth 10%.

Ball n Goal "Lower" Student Assessment Worksheet

Name: _____

DIRECTIONS: Circle the correct way of doing each skill.

Back of Worksheet

Back of Worksheet

3all n Goal "Higher" Student Assessment Worksheet

Name: _____

DIRECTIONS: Use this diagram to compare and contrast throwing underhand with throwing overhand. List the cues unique to throwing underhand on the lines under "Throwing Underhand." Use the lines in the middle (overlapping section) to list the cues that are similar to both throwing underhand and throwing overhand. List the cues unique to throwing overhand on the lines under "Throwing Overhand." Each line represents a cue. Each answer is worth 10 points. The passing grade is 80%.

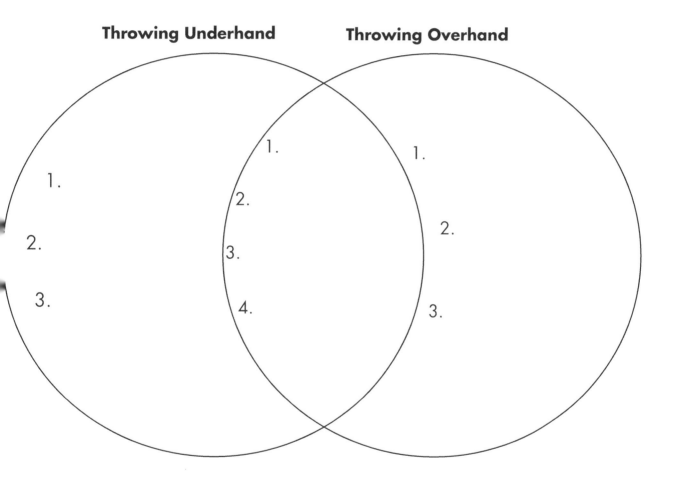

Throwing Underhand   **Throwing Overhand**

Throwing Underhand:
1.
2.
3.

Middle (overlapping):
1.
2.
3.
4.

Throwing Overhand:
1.
2.
3.

Back of Worksheet

Throwing Underhand   **Throwing Overhand**

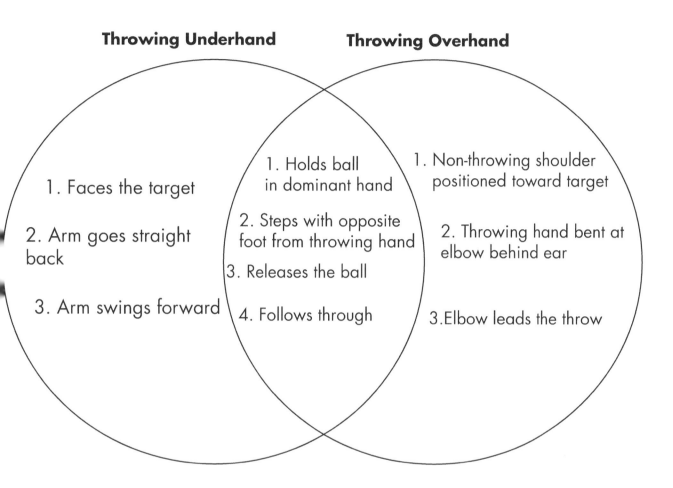

1. Faces the target

2. Arm goes straight back

3. Arm swings forward

1. Holds ball in dominant hand

2. Steps with opposite foot from throwing hand

3. Releases the ball

4. Follows through

1. Non-throwing shoulder positioned toward target

2. Throwing hand bent at elbow behind ear

3. Elbow leads the throw

Skill Concepts: Throwing, Catching, Volleying, Setting, Heading, Kicking

Standard: NASPE Standard 1 (Competency in motor skills)

Equipment: 2 goals, 3 balls per student, 4 cones

Set Up:

1. Place the goals on either side of the activity space, halfway down the "court."
2. Place cones in the center of the court, dividing the space into 2 halves.
3. Scatter half the balls in each side of the court.
4. Divide students into 2 teams as they enter the activity area.
5. Have each team sit in their half of the court.

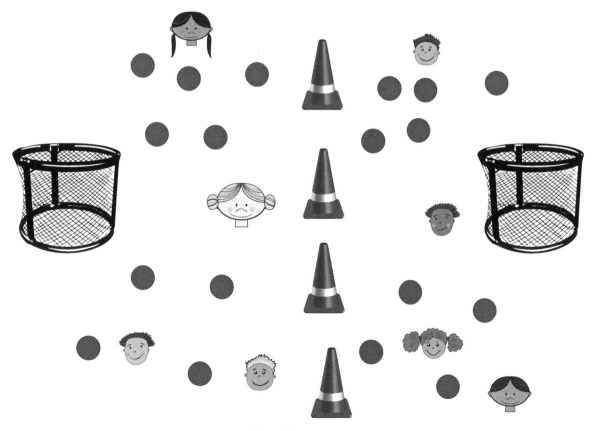

How To Play:

1. Instruct students from both teams to throw the balls on their side to the other side when you give the signal. They should try to get as many balls as possible into the other team's goal.

2. Tell students they are not allowed to step beyond the cone barrier line separating the 2 teams.

3. Allow students to get and throw balls out of the goal if they perform a physical fitness activity (5 sit-ups, self-toss/catch the ball 5 times, etc.). The student can only retrieve 1 ball at a time.

4. After 1 minute, signal to the students to stop throwing.

5. Count the balls on each side of the court. A ball on the floor is worth 1 point. A ball in the goal is worth 5 points.

6. The team with the least amount of points is the winner.

Check This Out:

1. Vary the types of throws: underhand, free style, etc.

2. Change the type of skill used to propel the ball. Students may try kicking, rolling, striking with hands, volleyball bumping, volleyball setting, soccer heading, and more.

Activity Modifications:

EASIER

1. Decrease the size of the playing field.

2. Move the goals to the front and middle of the field to make scoring goals easier.

3. Decrease the number of balls so students can track the equipment more easily.

4. Have students perform easier and/or a fewer amount of physical fitness activities before being allowed to get and throw a ball from the goal.

HARDER

1. Increase the size of the playing field.

2. Use the non-dominant hand to throw and/or non-dominant foot to kick.

3. Have students perform harder and/or more repetitions of physical fitness activities before being allowed to get and throw a ball from the goal.

Not in My Back Yard Teacher Assessment

DIRECTIONS: Students will demonstrate competency in motor skills by achieving a score of 2 or higher for each of the Not in My Back Yard Teacher Assessment skills.

1. Using the template below and your class roster, create and print your own personalized assessment form.

2. Observe each student while they are playing Not in My Back Yard to determine if the skill is performed correctly, using the rubric and listed cues for each skill to guide grading:

   - 1=Needs Improvement: cannot demonstrate the critical elements of the skill with cues from the teacher.

   - 2=Satisfactory: demonstrates the critical elements of the skill with cues from the teacher.

   - 3=Outstanding: demonstrates all of the critical elements of the skill without cues from the teacher.

3. Add comments as needed in the section provided.

Underhand Throwing

- Face target with ball in dominant hand.
- If student is capable of standing: Step with opposite foot towards the target (i.e., if throwing with right hand, step towards target with left foot).
- Use a pendulum arm motion with the throwing arm (i.e., like bowling).
- Follow through with the throwing hand pointing toward the target.

Overhand Throwing

- Point non-throwing side/shoulder to the target (for example, if right handed point left shoulder/side towards target).
- Bring throwing wrist of dominant hand back to ear with ball in hand.
- If student is capable of standing: Step with opposite foot towards target (i.e., if throwing with left hand, step towards target with right foot).
- Follow through: let the throwing arm come across the opposite side of body.

Kicking

- If student is capable of standing: Place non-kicking foot next to the ball.
- Contact ball in the middle with preferred foot.
- Use the inside of the preferred foot.
- Follow through: point-kicking foot toward target.
- Use a firm kick (with power) so the ball reaches the target.

Rolling

- Hold ball in dominant hand.
- If student is capable of standing: Step forward with the opposite foot.
- Bend at the knee (if standing) or waist (if sitting) to be closer to the ground.
- Swing arm holding the ball back.
- Swing the arm with the ball forward in front of the body.
- Let the ball roll out of the hand and onto the floor without the ball bouncing. The ball stays on the floor as it rolls.

TO PASS: Students must achieve a score of 2 or higher for each skill.

Student Name	Underhand Throwing	Overhand Throwing	Kicking	Rolling	Comments

Not in My Back Yard Student Assessment

DIRECTIONS: Students will demonstrate competency in motor skills by achieving a score of 70% or higher on the Not in My Back Yard Student Assessment Worksheet.

Lower Cognitive Functioning Students:

1. Give one copy of the appropriate worksheet (e.g., kicking and/or underhand throwing depending on the skill the student performed the most during the activity) and a crayon to each student.

2. After you read a sentence and the students follow along, tell the students to fill in the faces by drawing:

   - A "smile" to make a happy face if they agree (i.e., "Yes!").
   - A straight line if they are unsure or feel "So-so," or "OK."
   - A "frown" if they do not agree (i.e., "No").

3. Collect the papers and grade when the assessment is complete.

TO PASS: Each student should have a combination of at least 3 smiles (Happy/"Yes") or OK faces.

Higher Cognitive Functioning Students:

1. Give each student a Not in My Back Yard Higher Student Assessment Worksheet and a pencil.

2. Give students time to complete the worksheet and turn it back in for grading.

3. Use the rubric below to guide the grading of the worksheets.

TO PASS: Each student must achieve 70% or higher.

	1	2	3
Accuracy of Rating	Inaccurate	Somewhat Accurate	Very Accurate
Number of examples	0-1	2	3
Example descriptions	Poor descriptions	Good overall descriptions	Extremely descriptive
Correctness	0-1 are correct	2 are correct	All 3 are correct
Neatness	Not legible	Neat	Extremely neat
Spelling/grammar	Many errors	Some errors	Very few or no errors

0-10 = F (0-60%); 11-12 = D (61-71%); 13 = C (72-76%); 14-15 = B (77-87%); 16-18 = A (88-100%)

Notes:

Not in My Back Yard Lower Student Assessment Worksheet:

KICKING

Name: _____

| Yes! | So-so / OK | No |

1. I can PLANT my foot next to the ball.

2. I can use my foot as a PUTTER.

3. I can PUSH the ball with my foot to the target.

4. I am a good kicker.

Not in My Back Yard Lower Student Assessment Worksheet:

UNDERHAND THROWING

Name: _____

Yes!	So-so / OK	No

1. I face target with ball in my favorite hand

2. I step with opposite foot towards the target.

3. I bring my throwing arm back, then forward.

4. I follow through pointing to the target.

5. I am a good thrower.

Not in My Back Yard Higher Student Assessment Worksheet

DIRECTIONS: First, rate yourself on your skill performance in 1 of the skills listed below using the following rubric to guide your grading:

- 1 = Successful 0 to 24% of the time
- 2 = Successful 25% - 49% of the time
- 3 = Successful 50% - 74% of the time
- 4 = Successful 75% - 89% of the time
- 5 = Successful 90% - 100% of the time

Underhand Throwing: _____ Overhand Throwing: _____ Kicking: _____

Practice helps people improve their skills. Choose 1 skill and list and explain 3 examples that you will do outside of class to improve that skill. You will be graded using the rubric below. You need a score of 70% or higher to pass.

	1	2	3
Accuracy of Rating	Inaccurate	Somewhat Accurate	Very Accurate
Number of examples	0-1	2	3
Example descriptions	Poor descriptions	Good overall descriptions	Extremely descriptive
Correctness	0-1 are correct	2 are correct	All 3 are correct
Neatness	Not legible	Neat	Extremely neat
Spelling/grammar	Many errors	Some errors	Very few or no errors

0-10 = F (0-60%); 11-12 = D (61-71%); 13 = C (72-76%); 14-15 = B (77-87%); 16-18 = A (88-100%)

Skill Chosen: _____

1. 1st example to improve my skill:

2. 2nd example to improve my skill:

3. 3rd example to improve my skill:

Notes:

ACTIVITY #3: CRISS CROSS

Skill Concepts: Throwing, Catching

Standard: NASPE Standard 2 (Understands movement concepts)

Equipment: 1 goal, 1 polyspot per student, 1 ball per student

Set Up:

1. Place the goal in the center of the activity space.
2. Put the polyspots approximately 1 yard away from and around the goal.
3. Put 1 ball on top of each polyspot.

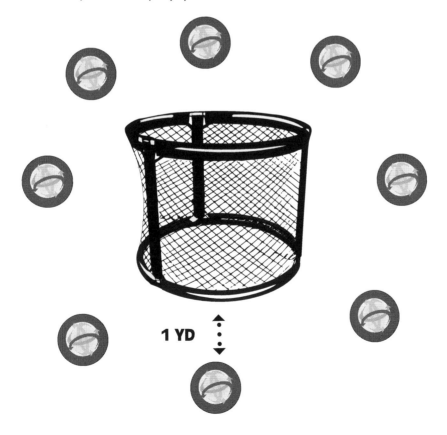

How To Play:

1. Have students sit on the polyspot as they enter the activity area, facing the goal.

2. Ask students to place the ball on their left side.

3. At your signal, have students reach with their right hand across their body to the left side to pick up the ball.

4. Once the ball is picked up with the right hand, have students make an infinity sign (sideways 8) from shoulder to shoulder.

5. Tell the students to keep their eyes on the ball while they make the infinity sign and to breathe normally.

6. Have the students create 3-5 infinity signs.

7. When the students are done with the last sign, have them turn their left shoulder toward the goal and throw the ball overhand into the goal, crossing the midline of their body (ie., students hold the ball in their right hand, cross the midline of the body, and release the ball by the left shoulder).

8. Have students safely retrieve the ball from the goal, sit back down on their polyspot, place the ball on their right side, and perform steps 3-7 using the left hand crossing over the right side.

Check This Out:

1. Have students perform the activity while in a kneeling or standing position.

2. Place students in pairs (distance determined by ability level). Students should play a game of catch, making sure they throw the ball across the midline of the body. On your signal, the student with the ball should throw it into the goal, making sure to cross the midline of the body when throwing.

Activity Modifications:

EASIER

1. Move the polyspots closer to the goal.

2. Instead of throwing the ball into the goal, allow students to roll the ball (making sure the ball still crosses the midline of the body).

3. Allow students to use 2 hands to hold and throw balls.

4. Let students choose to throw underhand or overhand into the goal.

HARDER

1. Have students sit, kneel, or stand with their backs facing the goal so they have to throw the ball over their shoulder into the goal.

2. Move the polyspots farther away from the goal.

Criss Cross Teacher Assessment

DIRECTIONS: Students will demonstrate an understanding of movement concepts by achieving a 4 or higher using the rating scale for each skill observed.

1. Using the template below and your class roster, create and print your own personalized assessment form.

2. Observe each student while they are playing Criss Cross to determine if the motor skills are performed correctly, using the rating scale and listed cues for each skill to guide grading and including comments as necessary:

   - 1 = Evident 0 to 24% of the time
   - 2 = Evident 25% - 49% of the time
   - 3 = Evident 50% - 74% of the time
   - 4 = Evident 75% - 89% of the time
   - 5 = Evident 90% - 100% of the time

Underhand Throwing into the Goal or to Partner:

- Faces target
- Steps with opposite foot from throwing hand (if student has the ability to step)
- Arm goes back
- Arm swings forward and releases the ball

Overhand Throwing into Goal or to Partner:

- Throwing wrist comes back to ear
- If student is capable of standing, steps with opposite foot towards target (i.e., if throwing with left hand, steps towards target with right foot)
- Arm leads with elbow when moving forward
- Ball is released
- Arm comes across the opposite side of body in a follow through

Catching:

- Keeps eye on ball
- Reaches arms towards ball
- Gives with ball as ball hits hands (brings ball into body)
- Puts pinkies together if ball is below waist
- Puts thumbs together if ball is above waist

OPTIONAL: Grade how successful the students were at each skill attempt.

TO PASS: Students must achieve a score of 4 or higher for each skill.

Student Name	Underhand Throwing	Catching	Overhand Throwing	Comments

Criss Cross Student Assessment

DIRECTIONS: The students will demonstrate an understanding of movement concepts by having at least 4 smiles (lower cognitive) or a score of 80% or higher (higher cognitive) on the Criss Cross Student Assessment Worksheet.

Lower Cognitive Functioning Students:

1. Make one copy of the Criss Cross Lower Student Assessment Worksheet per student.

2. Give each student a worksheet and a crayon to complete the worksheet.

3. After you read a sentence and the students follow along, tell the students to fill in the faces by drawing:

   - A "smile" to make a happy face if they agree (i.e., "Yes!").
   - A straight line if they are unsure or feel "So-so," or "OK."
   - A "frown" if they do not agree (i.e., "No").

4. Write the student's name in the space provided while they are answering the questions.

5. Collect the papers and grade when the assessment is complete.

TO PASS: Each student should have a combination of at least four (4) smiles (Happy/"Yes") or OK faces.

Higher Cognitive Functioning Students:

1. Give each student a Criss Cross Higher Student Assessment Worksheet and a pencil to complete the worksheet.

2. Give students time to complete the worksheet and turn it back in for grading.

3. Award 10 points for each correct answer.

TO PASS: Each student must achieve an 80% or higher.

Criss Cross Lower Student Assessment Worksheet

Name: _____

Yes!	So-so / OK	No

1. I use my EYES to watch the ball.

2. I REACH with my arms to get the ball.

3. I GIVE with the ball when it gets to my hands.

4. I have my PINKIES TOGETHER when catching a ball below my waist.

5. I have my THUMBS TOGETHER when catching a ball above my waist.

6. I am a good catcher.

Criss Cross Higher Student Assessment Worksheet

DIRECTIONS: Put the cues for each skill in order. The first cue for throwing is to be used as an example. Each correct answer is worth 10 points. You need an 80% to pass.

Throwing Underhand

CUE	NUMBER ORDER
Arm straight back behind body	1. Hold the ball in favorite (dominant) hand OR face target
Release the ball	2.
Arm swings forward	3.
Face target	4.
Hold the ball in favorite (dominant) hand	5.

Catching

CUE	NUMBER ORDER
Reach arms towards ball	1.
Put pinkies together if ball is below waist	2.
Keep eye on ball as it travels toward you	3.
Put thumbs together if ball is above waist	4.
Give with ball as it hits hands (bring ball into body)	5.

Back of Worksheet

DIRECTIONS: Put the cues for each skill in order. You need an 80% to pass.

Throwing Overhand

1. Hold the ball in favorite (dominant) hand OR face target
2. Face target OR hold the ball in favorite (dominant) hand
3. Bring arm straight back behind body
4. Swing arm forward
5. Release the ball

Catching

1. Keep eye on ball as it travels toward you
2. Reach arms towards ball
3. Give with ball as ball hits hands (bring ball into body)
4. Put pinkies together if ball is below waist OR Thumbs together if ball is above waist
5. Put thumbs together if ball is above waist OR Pinkies together if ball is below waist

ACTIVITY #4 : LAUNCH PAD

Skill Concepts: Depth perception

Standard: NASPE Standard 2 (Understanding movement concepts, principles, strategies and tactics)

Equipment: 1 goal, 1 GenMove ball per student, 1 polyspot per student, 1 beanbag for each lower cognitively functioning student, 1 large ball (basketball, playground ball, or volleyball) for each higher cognitively functioning student, 2-3 Hula-hoops (optional)

Set Up:

1. Place the goal in the center of the activity area.
2. Scatter polyspots throughout the activity area.
3. Place the GenMove ball and beanbag or large ball on each polyspot.
4. Have students sit on a polyspot as they enter the activity area (1 student per polyspot).

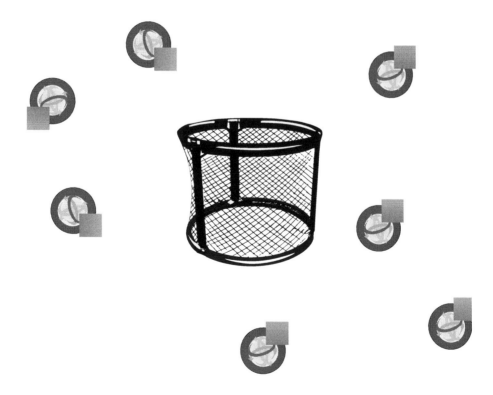

How To Play:

1. Instruct lower cognitively functioning students to place the beanbag on top of the GenMove ball, and higher cognitively functioning students to hold the Gen-Move ball on top of the large ball.

2. Have students hold the equipment at waist, chest, or shoulder level.

3. Give a signal for the students to release the ball in front of them (so both items fall to the ground at the same time) onto the polyspot, trying to launch the top item into the goal.

4. Have students safely retrieve their equipment and return to their polyspots.

5. Allow students to move their polyspots in any direction (based on where the object landed previously) in an attempt to successfully launch the item into the goal.

Check This Out:

1. MATH COMPONENT: Award points each time an item goes into the goal. Have the students calculate their own and/or the group's scores.

2. Scatter Hula-hoops around the area. Award 1 point for any item landing in the Hula-hoop and 2 points for an item landing in the goal.

Activity Modifications:

EASIER

1. If a student is not able to hold the equipment on his/her own, have a helper who can assist the student in holding the items before dropping them.

HARDER

1. PHYSICS COMPONENT: Have students explain why the smaller object was launched so high by the larger object. (ANSWER: This experiment is all about conservation of energy and momentum. When the balls are dropped together most of the momentum from BOTH balls is transferred to the small ball. Both the kinetic energy and the momentum of any moving object depends on its mass. If the smaller ball receives all the kinetic energy and momentum from the larger ball, it will bounce much higher than the original larger ball because it is so much lighter. Add to that the original energy and momentum in the smaller ball, and you get a bounce that is much greater than the sum of the two original bounces).

2. Use this experiment to demonstrate Chaos effects – small changes in the initial conditions (e.g., exactly how the two balls are held above one another) can cause large differences in the end results. Have students experiment with the placement of the balls over one another and drop the balls to see what the results yield.

3. After discussing energy and momentum, ask students to predict what they think will happen if the small ball is on the bottom. Have students perform the experiment and explain the results.

Launch Pad Teacher Assessment

DIRECTIONS: Students will demonstrate an understanding of movement concepts by achieving a score of 100% on the Launch Pad Teacher Assessment.

1. Using the template below and your class roster, create and print your own personalized assessment form.

2. Have students line up in a single file in front of you before exiting the activity space.

3. Before leaving the activity space, have each student correctly identify a sport that follows the same physics principle seen in the Launch Pad activity (i.e., for every action there is a an equal and opposite reaction).

4. Note on the assessment sheet whether each student correctly identifies a sport with the same principle. (Answers include any striking activities, including all racket sports, softball hitting, bowling [pins move when hit by ball], floor/field/ice hockey, billiards, and so on.)

5. If a student does not answer the question correctly, either:

    *   Ask again, giving hints as to sports that include the principle;

    *   Ask the student to "show me a sport" (and have a poster with pictures of different sports with and without the principle for them to point to); or

    *   Record the result on the assessment form and move on to the next student.

6. Add comments as needed.

TO PASS: Students must achieve a score of 100% (a check in a "Yes" box)

	Responded correctly on first attempt		Responded correctly on second attempt		
Student Name	Yes	No	Yes	No	Comments

Launch Pad Student Assessment

DIRECTIONS: The students will demonstrate an understanding of movement concepts by achieving a score of 80% or higher on the Launch Pad Student Assessment Worksheet.

Lower Cognitive Functioning Students:

1. Make one copy of the Launch Pad Lower Student Assessment Worksheet per student.

2. Give each student a worksheet and a crayon to complete the worksheet.

3. Collect the papers and grade using the Launch Pad Lower Student Assessment Worksheet ANSWERS when the assessment is complete. Each correct answer is worth 20 points.

TO PASS: Students must achieve a score of 80% or higher.

Higher Cognitive Functioning Students:

1. Make one copy of the Launch Pad Higher Student Assessment Worksheet per student.

2. Give each student a worksheet and a pen to complete the worksheet.

3. Collect the papers and grade using the rubric below.

TO PASS: Students must achieve a score of 80% or higher.

	1	2	3
Sport Skills	0 correct sport skills given	1 correct sport skill given	2 correct sport skills given
Description of sport skill principle	0 correct descriptions given	1 correct description given	2 correct descriptions given
Neatness	Not Neat	Neat	Extremely Neat
Sentence Structure	Few or none of the sentences are written properly	Some sentences are written properly	All sentences are written properly

0-7 Points = F (0-59%); 8 pts. = D (60-69%); 9 pts. = C (70-79%); 10 pts. = B (80-89%); 11-12 points = A (90-100%)

Notes:

Launch Pad Lower Student Assessment Worksheet

Name:_____

DIRECTIONS: Circle the activity that shows Newton's Third Law, "For every action there is an equal and opposite reaction."

Back of Worksheet

Launch Pad Lower Student Assessment Worksheet ANSWERS

Back of Worksheet

Launch Pad Higher Student Assessment Worksheet

Name: _____

DIRECTIONS: Today's experiment was about conservation of energy and momentum. When the balls were dropped together, most of the momentum from BOTH balls was transferred to the small ball. Both the kinetic energy and the momentum of any moving object depends on its mass. If the smaller ball receives all the kinetic energy and momentum from the larger ball, it will bounce much higher than the original larger ball because it is so much lighter. Add to that the original energy and momentum in the smaller ball and you get a bounce that is much greater than the sum of the two original bounces.

Think about 2 sport skills that use this principle. Write each skill in the space provided. Then explain the principle at work in the blank space provided (use the back of the paper as necessary). Write NEATLY and in full sentences. Each question is worth 20 points each and will be graded using the rubric below. You need an 80% to pass.

An example is given to you to follow.

You will be graded on the following:

	1	2	3
Sport Skills	0 correct sport skills given	1 correct sport skill given	2 correct sport skills given
Description of sport skill principle	0 correct descriptions given	1 correct description given	2 correct descriptions given
Neatness	Not Neat	Neat	Extremely Neat
Sentence Structure	Most or none of the sentences are written properly	Some sentences are written properly	All sentences are written properly

0-7 Points = F (0-59%); 8 pts. = D (60-69%); 9 pts. = C (70-79%); 10 pts. = B (80-89%); 11-12 points = A (90-100%)

EXAMPLE:

Sport Skill: Batting a ball

Newton's third law of physics can be seen when a baseball bat strikes a baseball. The bat applies a force to the ball, and the ball accelerates rapidly after being struck. The ball also applies a force to the bat. However, the mass of the ball is small compared to the mass of the bat, which includes the batter attached to the end of it. If you've ever seen a wooden baseball bat break into pieces as it strikes a ball, then you've seen firsthand evidence of the ball's force. Also, when a bat hits the ball, the baseball hits back. The batter feels a jolt running through his or her hands when the ball is struck.

1. Sport Skill #1: _____

Description of sport skill principle #1:

2. Sport Skill #2: _____

Description of sport skill principle #2:

Notes:

ACTIVITY #5: MODIFIED JAI ALAI

Skill Concepts: Throwing, Catching

Standard: NASPE Standard 3 (Participates regularly in physical activity)

Equipment: 2 goals, 1 ball, 1 scoop per student, pinnies for half the class

Set Up:

1. Place one goal on each side in the middle of the activity area.
2. As students enter the activity area, divide them into 2 teams, with one team wearing the pinnies.
3. Place the students wearing pinnies on one side of the court and the non-pinnie students on the other side of the court.
4. Give all students a scoop.
5. Flip a coin to determine which team gets the ball.

How To Play:

1. Students throw and catch the ball to one another using the scoop in an attempt to score a goal.

2. The rules of play should be modified (changed or omitted) as needed based on student ability level:

RULE	EASIER	HARDER
Court positions	Students stay in zones and play only their position as forwards and guards	Movement on the court is uninhibited, with students playing offense and defense as possession of the ball changes
Scoops	Allowed to use hands and/or scoop	Only use scoop
Goal Keeper	No goal keeper	1-2 goal keepers
Number of passes before shooting goal	Must pass 2-3 times	Must pass 3 or more times
Guarding	No guarding allowed	Guarding allowed
After a point is scored	Start ball at half court	Offensive team gets ball from goal line (like basketball)

Check This Out:

1. Limit the time students have possession of the ball.

2. Place students of similar abilities in corresponding positions on both teams.

Activity Modifications:

EASIER

1. Decrease the distance between goals (shorten the playing field).

2. Use Velcro paddles/balls.

HARDER

1. Increase the distance between goals (lengthen/widen the playing field).

Modified Jai Alai Teacher Assessment

DIRECTIONS: Students will demonstrate knowledge about participating regularly in physical activity by correctly answering an exit question (below).

1. Using the template below and your class roster, create and print your own personalized assessment form.

2. Have students line up in a single file in front of you before exiting the activity space.

3. Before leaving the activity space, ask each student to identify a sport s/he has tried or will try outside of school that requires throwing and catching an object.

4. Note on the assessment sheet if each student correctly identifies a throwing sport. If s/he does not answer the question correctly, either:

   • Ask the student again, giving hints as to sports that include throwing and catching;

   • Ask the student to "show me an activity that you will try" (and have a poster with pictures of different throwing sports for them to point to and name); or

   • Record the result on the assessment form and move on to the next student.

5. Students need to receive 100% (answer the question correctly) for a passing grade.

6. Add comments as needed.

TO PASS: Students must achieve a score of 100% (a check in a "Yes" box)

Student Name	Responded correctly on first attempt		Responded correctly on second attempt		Comments
	Yes	No	Yes	No	

Modified Jai Alai Student Assessment

DIRECTIONS: Students will demonstrate knowledge about participating regularly in physical activity by achieving a score of 80% or higher on the Modified Jai Alai Student Assessment Worksheet.

Lower Cognitively Functioning Students:

1. Give each student a piece of paper and crayons, and have students draw a picture of themselves participating in their favorite physical activity (it does not have to be throwing related).

2. Tell them that the physical activity can be something they do in school or at home (e.g., playing on the playground or hiking with Mom and Dad).

3. Make sure each student has his/her name printed on the assessment.

4. Collect the pictures at the end of the activity.

5. Evaluate students' work, assessing if they successfully chose a physical activity they do in school or at home.

Higher Cognitively Functioning Students:

1. Give each student the Modified Jai Alai Student Assessment Worksheet.

2. Give students time to complete and turn in the worksheet.

3. Use the Modified Jai Alai Student Assessment Worksheet ANSWERS to grade the student worksheets.

4. Make the assessment harder by removing the "Skill" and/or "Warm-Up Activities Box" cues.

TO PASS: Students must achieve a score of 80% or higher.

Modified Jai Alai Lower Student Assessment

Name: _____

DIRECTIONS: Draw a picture of yourself playing your favorite physical activity.

Back of Worksheet

Modified Jai Alai Higher Student Assessment

Name: _____

DIRECTIONS:

1. Identify the skill necessary to perform each sport or activity listed below. Use the words in the "Skill" box to help you. Choose the best answer for each sport/activity. (Hint: Muscular strength and cardiovascular endurance are used twice.)

2. Next, write the name of 1 warm-up activity to help a person prepare to play the sport/activity for the skill listed. Use the warm-up activities listed in the "Warm-Up Activities" box to help you (use each answer once).

3. Each correct answer is worth 20%. You need an 80% or higher to pass.

Skill	Warm-Up Activities
1. Flexibility	1. Push-ups
2. Muscular Strength	2. Pull-ups
3. Cardiovascular Endurance	3. Jogging
	4. Straddle stretches
	5. Jumping rope

Sport/Activity	Skill	Warm-Up Activity
Soccer		
Gymnastics		
Weight Training		
Basketball		
Shot Put		

Back of Worksheet

Modified Jai Alai Student Assessment Worksheet ANSWERS

DIRECTIONS:

1. Identify the skill necessary to perform each sport or activity listed below. Use the words in the "Skill" box to help you. Choose the best answer for each sport/activity. (Hint: Muscular strength and cardiovascular endurance are used twice.)

2. Next, write the name of 1 warm-up activity to help a person prepare to play the sport/activity for the skill listed. Use the warm-up activities listed in the "Warm-Up Activities" box to help you (use each answer once).

3. Each correct answer is worth 20%. You need an 80% or higher to pass.

Skill	Warm-Up Activities
1. Flexibility	1. Push-ups
2. Muscular Strength	2. Pull-ups
3. Cardiovascular Endurance	3. Jogging
	4. Straddle stretches
	5. Jumping rope

Sport/Activity	Skill	Warm-Up Activity
Soccer	Cardiovascular Endurance	Jogging or Jumping rope
Gymnastics	Flexibility	Straddle stretches
Weight Training	Muscular Strength	Push-ups or Pull-ups
Basketball	Cardiovascular Endurance	Jogging or Rope jumping
Shot Put	Muscular Strength	Push-ups or Pull-ups

ACTIVITY #6: MISSION IMPOSSIBLE

Skill Concepts: Spatial awareness, Rolling, Throwing, Catching, Kicking, Physical fitness, Hand dribbling

Standard: NASPE Standard 4 (Achieves and maintains a health-enhancing level of physical fitness)

Equipment: 2 goals, 1 ball per student, 1 roll of painter's tape, 1 foam noodle, 1 elastic fitness band, 5 cones, 7 laminated arrows (8.5" X 11"), 2 polyspots

Set Up:

1. Before you set up the obstacle course, determine the appropriate distance between each obstacle and between the set of 4 cones based on students' ability (generally, the closer the obstacles/cones are to one another, the easier the course). Make sure students will have enough space to maneuver through the course safely.

2. Place the cones in a zigzag pattern as directed in the diagram.

3. Put a polyspot in front of the first cone, designating the starting point.

4. Place a ball on top of the polyspot.

5. Tape the laminated arrows to the floor with painter's tape, using the diagram below. The arrows are visual cues to guide the students as they move through the cone pathway.

6. Place one of the goals on its side with the entrance in front of the last zigzag cone.

7. Place a cone in front of the exit of the goal that is placed on its side.

8. Place the foam noodle or elastic fitness band next to this cone.

9. Put one of the polyspots in front of the foam noodle/cone.

10. Place the other goal in an upright position in front of the polyspot.

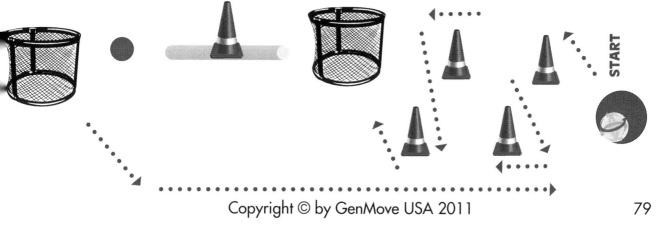

How To Play:

1. Have students line up in a single file behind the polyspot with the ball ("Start").

2. At your signal, have the first student pick up the ball and move as quickly as s/he can through the obstacle course. Student will:

   - Move through the set of 4 cones, following the arrows;
   - Crawl through the tunnel;
   - Reach the foam noodle/elastic fitness band, put the ball down, pick up the noodle or the band, perform 3 or more resistance exercises (the amount and type of exercise is dependent on equipment used and ability level), put the noodle/band back down by the cone, and pick up the ball;
   - Move to the polyspot near the upright goal and throw or kick (type of sport skill to be performed depends on ability level) the ball into the goal;
   - Retrieve the ball and return to the starting polyspot; and
   - Give the ball to the next student and move to the end of the line.

3. Repeat until all the players have had a chance to participate.

Check This Out:

1. Time how long the group takes to get through the course. Have students try to beat their scores each round.

2. Have many polyspots at varying distances around the upright goal, allowing students to choose which one to throw/kick from.

3. Have students perform other locomotor, sport or physical fitness skills through the cones and/or course. For example, they may run, move backwards, crab walk, bear walk (stomach toward ground), hand/foot dribble the ball, self-toss/catch the ball, do power jumps, and so on.

4. Have students design their own obstacle course.

Activity Modifications:

EASIER

1. Reduce the number of cones students move through at the beginning of the course.

HARDER

1. Add additional obstacles/fitness tasks based on students' abilities.
2. Have the students return through the obstacle course.
3. Move through the course backwards.

Mission Impossible Teacher Assessment

DIRECTIONS: Students will demonstrate knowledge that exercise and physical activity helps them achieve and maintain a health-enhancing level of physical fitness by achieving 100% on the Mission Impossible Teacher Assessment.

1. Using the template below and your class roster, create and print your own personalized assessment form.

2. Have students line up in a single file in front of you before exiting the activity space.

3. Before leaving the activity space, each student needs to correctly identify a health-related fitness activity that s/he did in class and the body part that it makes stronger. ANSWERS include:
   - arm resistance exercises (arms)
   - running through the cones (legs)
   - moving through the tunnel (arms)
   - throwing/kicking the ball into the goal (arms/legs)
   - hand/foot dribbling the ball through the course (arms/legs)

4. Note on the assessment sheet whether each student responded correctly. (Note: You want to assess whether each individual student understands physical activities help maintain fitness. Therefore, since many students tend to mimic one another, you may need to ask students to come up with something different than what the student in front of them said.)

5. If a student does not answer the question correctly, either:
   - Ask the student again, giving hints as to activities performed in class (demonstrate the movement of an activity like an arm resistance exercise);
   - Ask the student to "show me an activity that makes you fit" (and have a poster with pictures of the fitness skills performed along with non-fitness activities like sitting at a desk or lying in bed for them to point to);
   - Allow the students to come up with any activity that will make them fit (hiking, playing t-ball, etc.), or
   - Record the result on the assessment form and move on to the next student.

6. Add comments as needed.

TO PASS: Students must achieve a score of 100% (a check in a "Yes" box)

	Responded correctly on first attempt		Responded correctly on second attempt		
Student Name	Yes	No	Yes	No	Comments

Mission Impossible Student Assessment

DIRECTIONS: Students will demonstrate knowledge that exercise and physical activity helps them achieve and maintain a health-enhancing level of physical fitness by achieving a score of 80% or higher on the Mission Impossible Student Assessment Worksheet.

Lower cognitively functioning students:

1. Make one copy of the Mission Impossible Lower Student Assessment Worksheet per student.

2. Give each student 1 copy of the Mission Impossible Lower Student Assessment Worksheet and a crayon.

3. Ask the students, "Can you show (and or tell) me an exercise (and/or physical activity) that makes you fit?" Allow students to answer. Praise them if they were correct and add, "The best way to get fit is by doing exercises and using your muscles everyday!"

4. Tell the students to circle the exercises and physical activities that will make them fit. Allow students to color the pictures when they are finished circling the answers.

5. Answer any student questions before starting the activity.

6. Collect completed worksheets and grade using the Mission Impossible Lower Student Assessment worksheet ANSWERS.

TO PASS: Each student must achieve a score of 80% or higher. Each correct answer is worth 20 points.

Higher cognitively functioning students:

1. Give each student a copy of the Mission Impossible Higher Student Assessment Worksheet and a pencil.

2. Have students complete the worksheet and turn it in for grading.

3. Grade using the Mission Impossible Higher Student Assessment worksheet ANSWERS.

4. Create a harder assessment by asking students:

   - To list additional exercises and the muscles and fitness components the exercises address.

   - Which fitness component is missing? (ANSWER: Flexibility).

   - To list flexibility exercises and the muscles the exercises address.

TO PASS: Each correct answer is worth 10 points (10 points for listing a correct muscle and 10 points for identifying the correct fitness component). Each student must achieve a score of 80% or higher.

Notes

Mission Impossible Lower Student Assessment Worksheet

Name: _____

DIRECTIONS: Circle the exercises and sports that make you fit.

Back of Worksheet

Mission Impossible Lower Student Assessment worksheet ANSWERS

Notes:

Mission Impossible Higher Student Assessment Worksheet

Name:_____

DIRECTIONS: For each task, write at least 1 MAJOR, predominant muscle that is being exercised in the column labeled "Muscle". Then identify if the task improves/maintains muscular strength/endurance or cardiovascular endurance (choose only one answer) by placing an "X" in the correct column. (Hint: 3 answers are for muscular strength.)

Each correct answer is worth 10 points (10 points for the correct muscle and 10 points for identifying the correct fitness component). You need a score of 80% or better to pass.

Polyspot #	TASK	MUSCLE	MUSCULAR STRENGTH/ ENDURANCE	CARDIO ENDURANCE
1.	Running through the cones			
2.	Crab walking through the tunnel			
3.	Arm resistance exercises			
4.	Throwing/kicking the ball into the goal			
5.	Running back to the start			

Back of Worksheet

Mission Impossible Higher Student Assessment worksheet ANSWERS

DIRECTIONS: Students will demonstrate achievement in a health enhancing level of physical fitness by getting a score of 80% or higher on the Mission Impossible Higher Student Assessment Worksheet. Each correct answer is worth 10 points (10 points for the correct muscle and 10 points for identifying the correct fitness component).

Polyspot #	TASK	MUSCLE	MUSCULAR STRENGTH/ ENDURANCE	CARDIO ENDUR- ANCE
1.	Running through the cones	Heart		X
2.	Crab walking through the tunnel	Biceps, triceps, hamstrings, quadriceps	X	
3.	Arm resistance exercises	Heart	X	
4.	Throwing/kicking the ball into the goal	Biceps, triceps, forearm flexors, brachioradalis, brachialis, hamstrings, quadriceps	X	
5.	Running back to the start	Heart		X

ACTIVITY #7: SLING SHOT

Skill Concepts: Accuracy, Timing, Upper body strength

Standard: NASPE Standard 4 (Achieves and maintains a health-enhancing level of physical fitness)

Equipment: 2 goals, 1 Thera-Band (elastic exercise band) for every 3 students, 1 ball per student, 1 polyspot per student

Set Up:

1. Place both goals against the same wall approximately 5-7 yards from each other.

2. Group polyspots and balls into sets of 3. Put each set of polyspots approximately 1 yard apart and next to each other in a straight line. Place each group of polyspots approximately 3-4 yards apart from one another. The distance between the polyspots and the goals depends on the students' skill levels (see diagram).

3. Place a Thera-Band and 3 balls on the far left polyspot for every group.

4. Divide students into groups of 3 as they enter the activity area. Place each group at a set of polyspots with each member of the group sitting on a different polyspot.

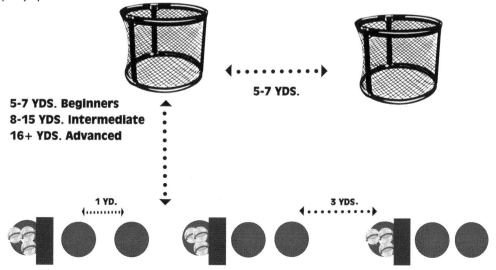

5-7 YDS. Beginners
8-15 YDS. Intermediate
16+ YDS. Advanced

5-7 YDS.

1 YD.

3 YDS.

How To Play:

1. Have the students on the right and left polyspots hold one end of the Thera-Band firmly to form a slingshot.

2. Instruct the student on the middle polyspot to place a ball in the center of the sling shot, hold it there while pulling back on the ball and Thera-Band, and release the ball/Thera band, shooting the ball towards the goal. Continue this activity until all 3 balls have been shot.

3. After every group has shot the 3 balls, have the students on the right retrieve the 3 balls and bring them back to the group.

4. Rotate positions. Have the student on the middle polyspot move to the right, the student on the left move to the middle, and the student on the right move to the left polyspot.

5. Continue the activity, repeating the steps above until all students have had the chance to go through at least 2 rotations.

Check This Out:

1. For safety, have the students slingshot the ball only on your command.

2. Remind the students holding onto the Thera-Band to do so TIGHTLY (use 2 hands if necessary) so the band does not slip out of their hands.

3. Integrate math by counting the balls in the goal and adding scores from each round.

4. Divide the class into 2 teams that compete against each other (most points scored in a round, most points scored by the end of the class, best trick shot, etc.).

Activity Modifications:

EASIER

1. Decrease the distance between the goals and polyspots.

2. Have a fourth person assisting the students needing it (either an extra set of hands holding onto the end of the Thera-Band, or helping to hold on to the ball and pulling the Thera-Band back to shoot it).

HARDER

1. Increase the distance between the goals and polyspots.

2. Tell the students they have to rebound the ball off the wall and into the goal.

Sling Shot Teacher Assessment

DIRECTIONS: Students will demonstrate knowledge that exercise and physical activity helps them achieve and maintain a health-enhancing level of physical fitness by achieving 100% on the Sling Shot Teacher Assessment.

1. Using the template below and your class roster, create and print your own personalized assessment form.

2. Have students line up in a single file in front of you before exiting the activity space.

3. Before leaving the activity space, each student needs to correctly identify an activity that will make their arms stronger.

4. Note on the assessment sheet whether each student responded correctly. (Note: You want to assess whether each individual student understands that physical activities help maintain fitness. Therefore, since many students tend to mimic one another, you may need to ask students to come up with something different than what the student in front of them said.)

5. If a student does not answer the question correctly, either:
   - Ask the student again in a different way;
   - Ask the student to "show me an activity that will make your arms stronger" (and have a poster with pictures of arm-strengthening activities along with non-arm-strengthening activities like sitting at a desk or lying in bed for them to point to); or
   - Record the result on the assessment form and move on to the next student.

6. Add comments as needed.

TO PASS: Students must achieve a score of 100% (a check in a "Yes" box)

Student Name	Responded correctly on first attempt		Responded correctly on second attempt		Comments
	Yes	No	Yes	No	

Sling Shot Student Assessment

DIRECTIONS: Students will demonstrate knowledge that exercise and physical activity helps them achieve and maintain a health-enhancing level of physical fitness by achieving a score of 80% or higher on the Sling Shot Student Assessment Worksheet.

Lower cognitively functioning students:

1. Give one copy of the Sling Shot Lower Student Assessment Worksheet and a crayon to each student.

2. Write the student's name at the top of the worksheet.

3. Ask the students to identify specific muscles:

   • "Can you point to a muscle in your arm?" Allow students point to a muscle in their arm. Praise them if they pointed to an arm muscle.

   • Then ask, "Can you point to a muscle in your leg?" Allow students point to a muscle in their leg. Praise them if they pointed to a leg muscle.

   • "How do you think we can make our muscles stronger?" Let students answer. Praise correct answers and tell them, "The best way to make our muscles stronger is by doing exercises and using our muscles everyday!"

4. Tell the students to draw a line with the crayon matching the body part "muscle" picture in the middle of the worksheet to the correct activity that strengthens that body part. An example is given on the worksheet for them to follow.

5. Collect completed worksheets and grade using the Sling Shot Lower Student Assessment Worksheet ANSWERS.

   TO PASS: Each student must correctly match a total of 4 pictures (20 points each).

Higher cognitively functioning students:

1. Give each student 1 copy of the Sling Shot Higher Student Assessment Worksheet and a pencil.

2. Students work in groups of 2-3 to complete the assignment.

3. Collect the papers when time is up and grade the worksheets using the rubric below.

TO PASS: Groups must achieve a score of 80% or higher.

	1	2	3	4
Number of exercises	0	1	2	3
Descriptions	Poor descriptions	Good overall descriptions	Very good descriptions	Extremely descriptive ideas
Correctness	No exercises are correct	1 exercise is correct	2 exercises are correct	All 3 exercises are correct
Neatness	Not legible	Neat	Very neat	Extremely neat
Spelling/grammar	Many errors	Some errors	Few errors	No errors

0-11: F (0-59%); 12-13: D (60-69%); 14-15: C (70-79%); 16-17: B (80-89%); 18-20: A (90-100%)

Notes:

Sling Shot Lower Student Assessment Worksheet

Name: _____

DIRECTIONS: Draw a line matching the muscle to the activity that makes that muscle stronger.

Back of Worksheet

Sling Shot Lower Student Assessment Worksheet: ANSWERS

Notes:

Sling Shot Higher Student Assessment Worksheet

DIRECTIONS: Your arm muscles were given a workout during the Sling Shot activity. Now you are going to work with your group to design 3 additional upper arm exercises that will increase upper body strength. You will be graded using the rubric below. You need a score of 80% or higher to pass.

	1	2	3	4
Number of exercises	0	1	2	3
Descriptions	Poor descriptions	Good overall descriptions	Very good descriptions	Extremely descriptive ideas
Correctness	No exercises are correct	1 exercise is correct	2 exercises are correct	All 3 exercises are correct
Neatness	Not legible	Neat	Very neat	Extremely neat
Spelling/grammar	Many errors	Some errors	Few errors	No errors

0-11: F (0-59%); 12-13: D (60-69%); 14-15: C (70-79%); 16-17: B (80-89%); 18-20: A (90-100%)

1. ACTIVITY #1:

2. ACTIVITY #2:

3. ACTIVITY #3:

Back of Worksheet

Notes:

ACTIVITY #8: CRAZY CHOPSTICKS

Skill Concepts: Cooperation, Teamwork, Concentration, Upper body strength, Eye-hand coordination

Standard: NASPE Standard 5 (Exhibits responsible personal and social behavior that respects self and others)

Equipment: 2 goals, 1 ball per student, 1 polyspot per student, 1 long foam noodle per student

Set Up:

1. Place the goals on opposite ends and in the middle of the activity area.
2. Scatter the polyspots throughout the general activity area.
3. Place 1 ball on each polyspot.
4. Place 2 foam noodles next to a ball/polyspot until all the noodles are placed.
5. Pair students into partners as they enter the activity space. Have each pair sit next to a foam noodle/ball/polyspot set.

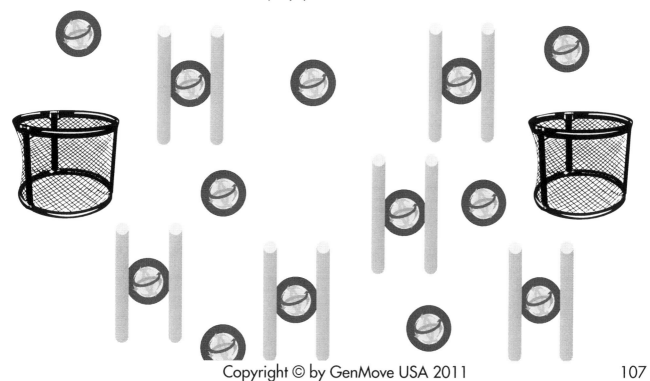

How To Play:

1. At your signal, have each student stand and pick up one foam noodle.

2. Tell the pairs of students that they must work cooperatively to use their individual foam noodles together as "chopsticks" to pick up the ball off the ground.

3. Once the ball is secured between the foam noodle chopsticks, have the pairs move to the goal as quickly as possible without dropping the ball or touching it with any body part.

4. Have the pairs work together to place their balls into the goal using only the foam noodle chopsticks.

5. Allow students to continue to the goal even if a ball drops or is touched.

6. When a ball is placed in the goal, have the pair find another ball on a polyspot and perform the activity again until all the balls are removed from the polyspots and placed into the goals.

Check This Out:

1. Add more balls in the activity area for extended play.

2. Divide the students into 2 teams, each with their own goal. The winner is the team with the most balls in their goal at the end of the round. You can make this harder by allowing the students to take balls out of each other's goals.

Activity Modifications:

EASIER

1. Allow students to use body parts to help keep the ball in the chopsticks.
2. Allow students to push the ball along the ground and into the goal using the chopsticks.

HARDER

1. Time the students to see how long it takes them to put all the balls into the goal. Have students try to beat their score each round.
2. Introduce consequences if a ball is dropped or touched with a body part.
   - Have students return to the starting point after a certain amount of drops/touches (e.g., 3 touches = start again). (Intermediate).
   - Have students return to the starting point after the first drop or touch (Advanced).
3. When students are raising and moving the ball to the goal, have them lift, hold, and move the ball at waist or chest level.
4. Have students perform this activity individually with each student bending 1 foam noodle in half to use as chopsticks.

Crazy Chopsticks Teacher Assessment

DIRECTIONS: Students will demonstrate responsible personal and social behavior that respects self and others in physical activity by achieving an 80% on the Crazy Chopsticks Teacher Assessment.

1. Using the template below and your class roster, create and print your own personalized assessment form.

2. Observe each student while they are playing Crazy Chopsticks.

3. Determine if the students "exhibit responsible personal and social behavior that respects self and others in physical activity settings," by checking YES or NO for each statement in the checklist.

4. Each YES answer receives 20 points.

5. Students need to receive 80% for a passing grade.

6. Add comments as needed.

Student Name	Showed willingness to work with partner		Supported partner when performing activity		Willing to work with given partner		Did not put self down or criticize self		Was courteous to other classmates while performing activity		Comments
	Yes	No	Yes	No	Yes	No	Yes	No	Yes	No	

Crazy Chopsticks Lower Student Assessment

DIRECTIONS: The students will demonstrate responsible personal and social behavior that respects self and others in physical activity by achieving an 80% or higher on the Crazy Chopsticks Student Assessment Worksheets.

Lower cognitively functioning students:

Materials:

- Crayons and 1 Crazy Chopstick Lower Student Assessment Worksheet per student.

The Assessment:

1. Tell the students to use the crayons to circle the pictures where people are showing respect (good manners) to each other. Students may then color in all the pictures.

2. Display the "good manners" pictures in the classroom and/or have the students bring the pictures home to show their parents.

Variation

Materials:

- 1 Crazy Chopstick Lower Student Assessment Worksheet, 1 safety scissor, 1 blank piece of 8.5" x 11" paper, and crayons for every student, plus 1 bottle of glue for every 2-3 students

The Assessment:

1. Tell the students to use the crayons to circle the pictures where people are showing respect (good manners) to each other. Students may then color in all the pictures.

2. Have the students use the scissors to cut the colored-in pictures.

3. Tell the students to use the glue to paste ONLY the pictures where people are showing respect (good manners) to each other onto the blank paper.

TO PASS: Each correct answer is worth 20 points. Student must correctly identify 4 respect (good manners) pictures in order to achieve a score of 80% or higher.

Higher cognitively functioning students:

1. Divide students into groups of 2-3. Give each group a copy of the Crazy Chopstick Higher Student Assessment Worksheet and a pencil.

2. Have each group complete the worksheet and return it for grading.

3. Use the rubric below to grade the worksheets.

TO PASS: Students must achieve a score of 80% or higher.

	1	2	3	4
Number of ideas	0-1	2	3	4
Descriptions	Poor descriptions	Good overall descriptions	Very good descriptions	Extremely descriptive ideas
Correctness	0-1 modifications are correct	2 modifications are correct	3 modifications are correct	All modifications are correct
Neatness	Not legible	Neat	Very neat	Extremely neat
Spelling/grammar	Many errors	Some errors	Few errors	No errors

0-11: F (0-59%); 12-13: D (60-69%); 14-15: C (70-79%); 16-17: B (80-89%); 18-20: A (90-100%)

Crazy Chopsticks Lower Student Assessment Worksheet

NAME: _____

DIRECTIONS: Circle the pictures where people are showing respect (good manners) to each other. Then color in the pictures.

Back of Worksheet

Crazy Chopsticks Lower Student Assessment Worksheet: ANSWERS

Notes:

Crazy Chopstick Higher Student Assessment Worksheet

DIRECTIONS: Some of your classmates (and maybe even YOU!) found playing Crazy Chopsticks too easy or too hard. Since it's important to respect differences, you and your group are going to create a total of 4 activity modifications (2 easy and 2 difficult) for the Crazy Chopsticks game played in class. Use the back of this sheet if you need more space. You will be graded using the rubric below. You need a score of 80% or higher to pass.

	1	2	3	4
Number of ideas	0-1	2	3	4
Descriptions	Poor descriptions	Good overall descriptions	Very good overall descriptions	Extremely descriptive ideas
Correctness	0-1 modifications are correct	2 modifications are correct	3 modifications are correct	All modifications are correct
Neatness	Not legible	Neat	Very neat	Extremely neat
Spelling/grammar	Many errors	Some errors	Few errors	No errors

0-11: F (0-59%); 12-13: D (60-69%); 14-15: C (70-79%); 16-17: B (80-89%); 18-20: A (90-100%)

1. EASIER MODIFICATION #1: _____
   _____
   _____
   _____

2. EASIER MODIFICATION #2: _____
   _____
   _____
   _____

3. HARDER MODIFICATION #1: _____
   _____
   _____
   _____

4. HARDER MODIFICATION #2: _____
   _____
   _____

Back of Worksheet

Notes:

ACTIVITY #9: GENMOVE EXPRESS

Skill Concepts: Upper body strength, Cooperation, Aiming (Accuracy)

Standard: NASPE Standard 5 (Exhibits responsible personal and social behavior)

Equipment: 2 goals, 1 ball per student, 1 parachute (VARIATION for higher cognitively functioning students: 1 large towel per pair of students)

Set Up:

If using the parachute:

1. Place parachute in the middle of the activity area.
2. Position the goals approximately 3 yards away from and on either side of the parachute.
3. Place the balls in a pile off to the side of the parachute.

If using towels:

1. Divide the towels between the goals, placing half the towels approximately 4 yards away from and around each goal.
2. Place 2 balls on each towel.

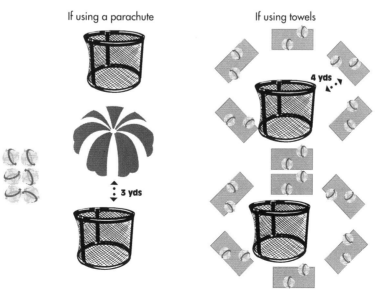

If using a parachute   If using towels

4 yds

3 yds

121

How To Play:

If using the parachute:

1. Have students stand around the parachute, holding onto the edges.
2. Signal students to gently move their arms up and down, shaking the parachute ("making waves").
3. Place 1 ball onto the parachute (more can be added after the students practice with the first ball).
4. Tell the students to work together in raising the parachute to launch the ball into one of goals.

If using towels:

1. Place students in pairs (or in teams of 3-4 if using an extra large towel or bed sheet) with each pair holding onto the ends of the towel.
2. Signal students to place 1 ball onto the towels (more can be added after the students practice with the first ball).
3. Tell the students they must work with their partners in using the towel to launch the ball into the goal.

Check This Out:

1. After the students practice getting 1 ball from the parachute into a goal, put numerous balls in the middle of the parachute. Have students work together to get as many of the balls as they can into either goal.
2. MATH INTEGRATION: Award 1 point for each ball staying in a goal.

Activity Modifications:

EASIER

1. Use beanbags.

2. Scatter Hula-hoops (and/or boxes) around the parachute. Award points for a beanbag and/or ball landing in a goal, Hula-hoop, or box.

3. Decrease the distance between the goal and parachute/towels.

HARDER

1. Increase the distance between goals and parachute/towels.

2. Make students using a towel bounce the ball once (and only one time) before it goes into the goal.

3. Have beanbags worth "X" amount of points and balls worth a different amount of points.

4. Have goals, Hula-hoops and boxes each worth a different amount of points.

5. Ask the students to calculate different computations (e.g., subtract the number of balls in the goals from the number of balls in the Hula-hoops).

GenMove Express Teacher Assessment

DIRECTIONS: Students will demonstrate responsible personal and social behavior that re spects self and others in physical activity by achieving an 80% on the GenMove Expres Teacher Assessment.

1. Using the template below and your class roster, create and print your own per-sonalized assessment form.

2. Observe each student while they are playing GenMove Express.

3. Determine if the students "Exhibit responsible personal and social behavior that respects self and others in physical activity settings," by checking YES or NO for each statement in the checklist.

4. Award each YES answer 20 points. Students need to receive 80% for a passing grade.

5. Add comments as needed.

Student Name	Showed willingness to work with classmates or partner		Supported classmates or partner when performing activity		Willing to work with class-mates or given partner		Did not put self down or criticize self		Was courteous to other class-mates while performing activity		Comments
	Yes	No	Yes	No	Yes	No	Yes	No	Yes	No	

124　　　　　　　　Copyright © by GenMove USA 2011

GenMove Express Student Assessment

DIRECTIONS: Students will demonstrate responsible personal and social behavior that respects self and others in physical activity by achieving an 80% on the GenMove Express Student Assessment Worksheet.

Lower cognitive functioning students:

1. Make one copy of the GenMove Express Lower Student Assessment Worksheet per student.

2. Give each student a worksheet and a crayon to complete the worksheet.

3. After you read a sentence and the students follow along, tell the students to fill in the faces by drawing:

   - A "smile" to make a happy face if they agree (i.e., "Yes!").
   - A straight line if they are unsure or feel "So-so," or "OK."
   - A "frown" if they do not agree (i.e., "No").

4. Write the student's name in the space provided while they are answering the questions.

5. Collect the papers and grade when the assessment is complete.

TO PASS: Each student should have a combination of at least four (4) smiles (Happy/"Yes") or OK faces.

Higher cognitive functioning students:

1. Make 1 copy of the "GenMove Express Higher Student Assessment Worksheet" per student.

2. Give each student a worksheet and a pen to complete the worksheet.

3. Collect the papers and grade when the assessment is complete.

TO PASS: Each student must achieve an 80% or higher on the GenMove Express Higher Student Assessment Worksheet.

Notes:

GenMove Express Lower Student Assessment Worksheet

Name: _____

Yes!   So-so / OK   No

1. I tried hard in class today.

2. I did well in the activity.

3. I liked working with my classmates.

4. I listened to and obeyed the rules.

5. I worked well with my classmates.

Back of Worksheet

GenMove Express Higher Student Assessment Worksheet

YOUR NAME: _____   PARTNER'S NAME: _____

DIRECTIONS: Answer the following 5 questions NEATLY and in full sentences, regarding you and your partner's performance in today's class. Each question is worth 20 points and will be graded using the rubric below. You need an 80% to pass.

Breakdown of the 20 Points per question	Content
15	The example given demonstrates responsible personal and social behavior.
2.5	The question is answered in a full sentence.
2.5	The response is neatly written.

1. Give 1 example of how your partner supported you during the activity.

2. Give 1 example (different than the answer above) of how you supported your partner.

3. Give 1 example of what you and your partner did when you were successful.

4. Give 1 example of what you and your partner did when you were not successful.

5. Give 1 example of how you helped each other when mistakes were made.

Back of Worksheet

Notes:

ACTIVITY #10 : WAR OF THE WORLDS

Skill Concepts: Throwing, Catching, Offensive/defensive strategy, Striking

Standard: NASPE Standard 6 (Values physical activity for health, enjoyment, challenge, self expression, and/or social interaction)

Equipment: 24 Hula-hoops, 3 or more cones (dividing the activity space into 2), 30 balls, 20 bowling pins (or similar items to knock down), 8 foam noodles (or similar soft striking implement – if not available, students may use hands), portable stereo and War of the Worlds soundtrack or other music, 2 goals

Set Up:

1. Place one polyspot in each of the 4 corners of the activity space.

2. Build 1 Hula-hoop sculpture over each polyspot. The polyspot is a visual cue so students know where to rebuild the Hula-hoop structure if it gets knocked down. A Hula-hoop structure is made of 6 hoops arranged in the following manner:

   • One Hula-hoop on the ground as the base.

   • Two Hula-hoops standing on edge on either side inside the base Hula-hoop, leaning against each other.

   • Two Hula-hoops standing on edge on the other sides inside the base Hula-hoop.

   • One Hula-hoop over the top, securing the Hula-hoop structure.

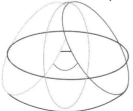

3. Place 3 or more cones in the center of the activity space to divide the space in half.

4. Put the goals at opposite ends and in the middle of activity space.

5. Scatter 15 balls in each half of the activity space.

6. Place 10 bowling pins throughout the general space in each half.

7. Place 4 foam noodles in each half of the activity space.

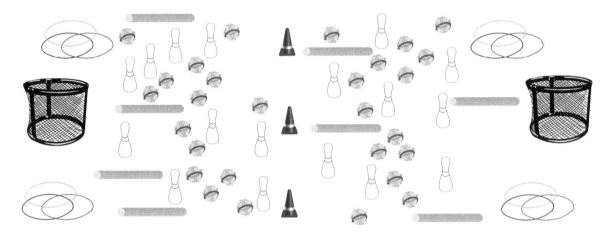

How to Play:

1. Divide the class into two teams, the "Earthlings" (Good) and the "Aliens" (Evil), who will battle in the War of the Worlds.

2. Explain that students will earn points by knocking down Hula-hoop structures and pins and getting balls into the goals. The objective is to be the team with the most points at the end of the class.

   • The Hula-hoop structures represent headquarters (Earthling's homes vs. spaceships).

   • The bowling pins represent the armies (Armed forces vs. Tripods).

   • The balls (representing Earthling bullets and Alien lasers) are thrown in order to knock down the bowling pins and Hula-hoop structures.

   • The foam noodles (representing shields on both sides) are used to knock away the balls, preventing them from hitting the bowling pins and Hula-hoop structures.

   • The goals represent the ultimate power. A ball landing in a goal is worth 10 points.

3. Allow the students to develop strategies, such as choosing the blockers (defense) and the attackers/throwers (offense) based on ability levels.

4. Start the music. Have students throw the balls, trying to knock down the bowling pins and Hula-hoop structures and to get the balls into the opposing team's goal, all while protecting their pins and Hula-hoops by using the foam noodles

and/or their hands to knock away balls thrown from the other team.

5. Do not allow students to cross the cones to the other team's side.

6. After 1-2 minutes of play (or if both structures and all the bowling pins are knocked down on one side), signal the students to stop. Each pin knocked down = 1 point; a Hula-hoop structure knocked down = 5 points for the team who knocked it down; each ball in the goal for the team who put it there = 10 points. The team with the most points wins the game.

Check This Out:

1. Change the types of throws to underhand, free style, etc.

2. Change the type of skill used to propel the ball to kicking, striking with hand, etc.

3. Allow students to get and throw balls out of the goal if they perform a physical fitness activity (e.g., 5 sit-ups, self-toss/catch the ball 5 times, etc.). The student can get only 1 ball at a time.

Activity Modifications:

Easier

1. Decrease the size of the playing field.

2. If using 2-liter plastic bottles as "bowling pins," stand them up using the cap as the base, allowing bottles to be knocked over more easily.

3. Move the Hula-hoop structures to the front and middle of the field to make them easier to knock down.

4. Have students use the noodles as cannons to launch balls rather than as striking implements.

5. Decrease the number of balls to make it easier for the students to track the equipment.

Harder

1. Increase the size of the playing field.

2. Have students throw with their non-dominant hand.

War of the Worlds Teacher Assessment

DIRECTIONS: Students will understand physical activity should be valued for health, enjoyment, challenge, self-expression, and/or social interaction by achieving a score of 100% on the War of the Worlds Teacher Assessment.

1. Using the template below and your class roster, create and print your own personalized assessment form.

2. Have students line up in a single file in front of you before exiting the activity space.

3. Before leaving the activity space, ask each student to give an example of a physical activity s/he values for (choose only one value per student):
   - Health benefits;
   - Enjoyment;
   - Challenge;
   - Self-expression; or
   - Social interaction.

4. Note on the assessment sheet whether each student gives a correct example of the value given. If a student does not give a correct example, either:
   - Ask for an example of a different value (e.g., if the original question was "Give me an example of a physical activity you value for health benefits," the second question would be "Give me an example of a physical activity you value for social interaction");
   - Ask the student to "Show me an activity that is valued for health benefits" (have a poster with pictures of different activities for them to point to for each value); or
   - Record the result on the assessment form and move on to the next student.

5. Students need to receive 100% (answer the question correctly) for a passing grade.

6. Add comments as needed.

TO PASS: Students must achieve a score of 100% (a check in a "Yes" box)

Student Name	Responded correctly on first attempt		Responded correctly on second attempt		Comments
	Yes	No	Yes	No	

War of the Worlds Student Assessment

DIRECTIONS: Students will understand physical activity should be valued for health, enjoyment, challenge, self-expression, and/or social interaction by achieving a score of 50% on the War of the Worlds Lower Student Assessment Worksheet or 80% on the War of the Worlds Higher Student Assessment Worksheet.

Lower cognitive functioning students:

1. Have students play a matching game to find all the matching pairs of cards.

2. Make one copy of the cards for every student (or for every 2 students if the students' ability level affords 2 students playing against each other).

3. Copy, cut out, and shuffle all the War of the Worlds Lower Student Assessment Cards, keeping sets together.

4. Place the cards face down on the table in front of the students (or pair of students) in a 4-card by 4-card square formation.

5. Have students select two of the cards by flipping the cards over revealing the pictures. (Pairs of students take turns selecting two cards.)

6. Remove the cards if both cards are the same. If they are different, flip them back over so the pictures cannot be seen.

7. Tell students that the game is over when all the cards have been matched. The winner (if you choose) is the student with the most paired cards.

8. Make the game more difficult by matching the picture to the word of the activity, or by adding more pictures.

TO PASS: Students must have matched at least half the cards.

Higher cognitive functioning students:

1. Make 1 copy of the War of the Worlds Die for every group of 2-3 students.

2. Cut out and tape together each Die.

3. Make 1 copy of the War of the Worlds Higher Student Assessment Worksheet for each student.

4. Place students in groups with 2-3 students in each group. Number the students in consecutive order (one student is numbered "1," the next "2," etc.).

5. Give each group 1 die and each student a worksheet and a pencil.

6. Have the student numbered "1" in each group roll the group's die.

7. Have each student in the group:

   a. Write the physical activity "value word" in the space provided for that roll on his/her own worksheet (see the worksheet).

   b. Finish the sentence on the worksheet, giving an example of the physical activity value shown on the die. For example, if the word "Health" were rolled, each student would write his/her own example of the physical activity related to that value: "I value physical activity because IF I EXERCISE EVERY DAY, MY HEART WILL GET STRONGER, PREVENTING ME FROM HAVING A HEART ATTACK." Tell students not to share answers.

8. After each student in the group has written a sentence, have the next numbered student roll the die (in this example, student numbered "2") with students performing the same steps listed above until all students have rolled the die and all sentences have been written. (It does not matter if the same word comes up more than once.)

9. Collect and grade papers.

TO PASS: Students receive 20 points for each correct example of the word written in a sentence (you can decide to create a rubric to grade students on grammar, spelling, sentence structure, etc.). Students must receive a score of 80% or higher to pass.

War of the Worlds Lower Student Assessment Cards

Back of Worksheet

War of the Worlds Die

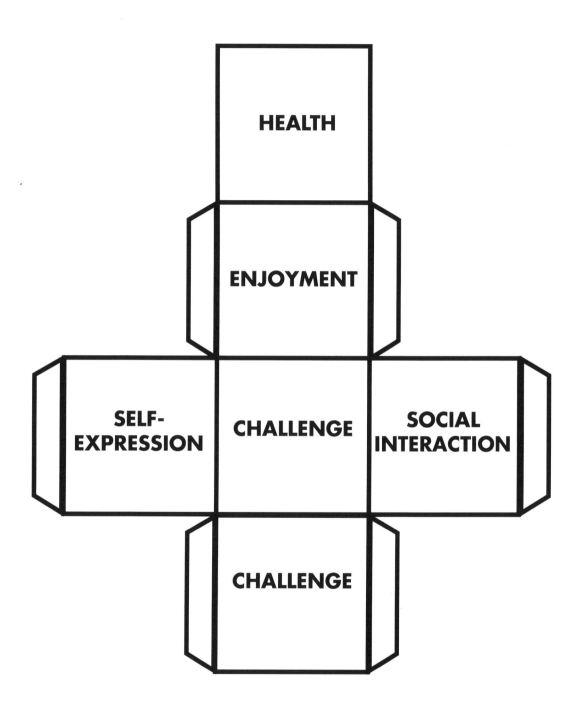

Back of Worksheet

War of the Worlds Higher Student Assessment Worksheet

DIRECTIONS:

1. Roll the die.
2. Write the word in the space on your worksheet.
3. Finish the sentence on your worksheet, giving an example of the physical activity value shown on the die (use the back of the worksheet if you need more room).
4. Do not look at each other's answers.

You will receive 20 points for each correct example of the word written in a sentence. You need a score of 80% or higher to pass.

EXAMPLE:

1. Health: I value physical activity because IF I EXERCISE EVERY DAY, MY HEART WILL GET STRONGER, PREVENTING ME FROM HAVING A HEART ATTACK.

Your turn:

1. _____: I value physical activity because _____
   _____
   _____

2. _____: I value physical activity because _____
   _____
   _____

3. _____: I value physical activity because _____
   _____
   _____

4. _____: I value physical activity because _____
   _____
   _____

5. _____: I value physical activity because _____
   _____
   _____

Back of Worksheet

For more fun, health-enhancing programs and activities, visit
www.genmoveusa.com

Made in the USA
Columbia, SC
06 September 2024

41964897R00080